Corridors

Poems and prose by
Cliff Britten

authorHOUSE®

AuthorHouse™
1663 Liberty Drive
Bloomington, IN 47403
www.authorhouse.com
Phone: 1-800-839-8640

© 2012 by Cliff Britten. All rights reserved.
Inside art illustrations and front cover photograph by Clifford Britten

No part of this book may be reproduced, stored in a retrieval system, or transmitted by any means without the written permission of the author.

First published by AuthorHouse   01/06/2012

ISBN: 978-1-4678-7746-6 (sc)
ISBN: 978-1-4678-7745-9 (ebk)

Printed in the United States of America

Any people depicted in stock imagery provided by Thinkstock are models, and such images are being used for illustrative purposes only.
Certain stock imagery © Thinkstock.

This book is printed on acid-free paper.

Because of the dynamic nature of the Internet, any web addresses or links contained in this book may have changed since publication and may no longer be valid. The views expressed in this work are solely those of the author and do not necessarily reflect the views of the publisher, and the publisher hereby disclaims any responsibility for them.

List Of Contents

Gift 1

Magnitude 9 3

Amazon in space 4

Bag lady 6

Brittle 8

Confusion 10

Daddy dearest 14

Rock 16

Trust me.. 17

Madman 18

Good days 21

Settle the Tab 22

Mount Pleasant.. 24

Do you like my shoes? 27

The need 29

Sleep 31

Last poem of sorts.. 32

Therapy 35

Summer Time 36

The Witch... 38

Sailor 42

Rules 45

The boot wearer 46

It's so bad 47

Woman act 48

Question 50

Totem Pole 51

6-15 pm 55

I am London 56

Boredom 59

Devil of a decision 63

Girls I knew	64
Watchmen	65
Flower	68
Don't worry	70
Living	72
Thinking	76
Phone call	77
Comedown	78
Prop	79
Entrenched	80
Night Visitor	82
Physicality	85
The speed of life	88
Warning	89
Register	90
Velux	91
The Bell	92
Ketamine (my special friend)	94
Dylan	99
Sometimes	100
To write	101
In Chicago	102
Meeting	104
Showtime	105
Kiln	107
Balloon	108
Snow	109
Babies and Nazis	110
Are you okay?	112
The lonely mask	113
Shortlist	115
Incongruous	116
10-second symmetry	117

This book is dedicated to all the people who have listened to my poems, over the phone and in private conversations. It is thanks to their encouragement and help that this book exists.

All I ever wanted and all I ever hoped for was just one of my poems to touch a nerve.

There may well be happy endings but they all stem from sad beginnings.

Gift

We have fallen in love

You and I

And as a token of this

I offer you my severed arm

Flesh torn and gouged from bone with blunt scissors

Bone cut through and splintered by rusty saw

Bloodied wound tended

With crude alcohol and fire to seal

Take it

This is in lieu

Of any future pain we may feel

Cliff Britten

Magnitude 9

Awoke this morning

To an outrage

Ten thousand dead

And spiralling

In a flash

The muddy hand of God

Swatted Japan

A tremor, a wave

And all this

Humanity

Shattered

In Biblical portrait

A mass of tears

Man's endeavour

Plundered

Like a stolen memory

The earth had cracked a

Huge smile

Under the ocean

But no one else laughed

Cliff Britten

Amazon in space

We met in space

On a bench

Thighs touched

And then remained

Touched

Frightened to

Lose that pressure

We spoke for hours

About pills and flowers

I was locked

In your emerald gaze

And cockney phrase

You were

Rigor mortis

Gorgeous

Techno and chemicals

Combined

Hearts pounded

Planes thundered

Corridors

I wondered

If you felt mine

You wanted to

Make shapes in space

We stood

You towered above me

Amazon woman

Three inches more

A tall order

We stayed together

In a lovers clinch

6 months

For every inch

Cliff Britten

Bag lady

I saw an old, cold lady in Victoria

Grey hair, pony tail. bent double

Shuffling along, staring at the floor, no choice

Struggling, dirty, exhausted, but intent

On carrying a huge red and white checked laundry bag

Containing her life

Every step an enormous effort

Every corner a new home

But she was going somewhere

Dragging that bag

Dragging, dragging, dragging

Every ten steps or so she would stop

Worn out, catch her breath

Recovered, she resumes

Pulling that monster, that bag

So important to her

I wondered what was in it

I wanted to explore that bag

To reveal the jigsaw of her life

Corridors

I wondered if the size of that huge bag

That burden she carried

Reflected all the emotional baggage

She had stowed away over the years

And how that too had weighed her down

"Leave it behind" I wanted to shout

"Leave it, leave it"

But then I realised I have a

Blue and white striped laundry bag

Very similar

Brittle

Falling, falling, falling

Leaf in autumn

Nothing to hold onto

Or hold me anymore

Spiralling down towards the floor

Roots that held me once

Have dried

I tried to hold I tried and tried

But then

They snapped

My life confused

No longer mapped

Cast adrift from the

Family tree

Blown and brittle

Solitary

I feel my loss

And start to waver

No hands to hold

Or lips to savour

Corridors

The veins of sap and life

I knew, they still remain

But I have been removed

That one-piece, me, devoid of food

So weightless,

I can't reach the ground

Unattached

An open wound

In a void

Just in the air

Sick and dying

Beyond repair

What then if I reach the ground

Will a new tree

Be there that's sound

For me to find

And then re—grow?

Or will I find a breeze

And blow

Confusion

I have a bad habit

Of hurting people

    People I love, people I like

People I need

    I don't mean it

But it recurs

Something happened to me

Swept me up

At some point

    Into this turmoil

And I don't know

What it was

But it still haunts

It must have been bad

Because I'm all messed up

I see couples all the time

Watch them kiss in the street

Hold hands

It seems unreal

Corridors

Vile sometimes

A temporary phase

                    Believe me

It will all end in tears

I can't love right now

                    Maybe never

I go through the motions

People say to me

That I am a good lover

That I am unselfish

                    That I am this

                    That I am that

All great reviews

Critical acclaim

But they don't get it

It's a cinch

I am just doing what I want

Not what they want

It's not about them

I do what pleases me

Just so happens they like it

                    I can sail to the moon

So I am selfish, selfish,

        Selfish

But I do sort of care

Even though

        Love and sex

Don't mix in my bowl

I have loved once

In a way I thought

Was right

I was unselfish,

But still lost it all

Contrary to that

        Self-centered

I became

A roaring success

If you are confused

Imagine how I feel

        I wish sex never existed

Why did you do it God?

You fucked up there

Corridors

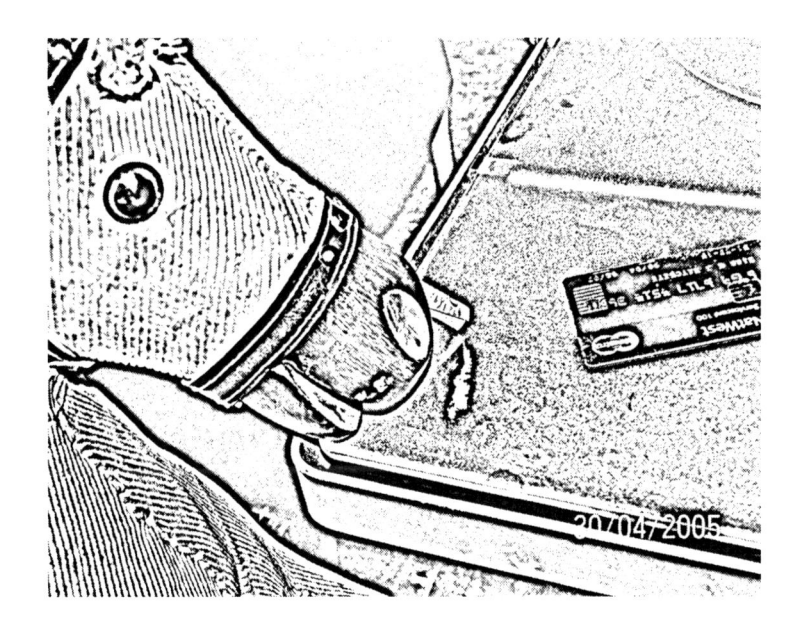

Cliff Britten

Daddy dearest

He never says much

Unless it's what horse

Has a chance

In the 3-30

Or about bad luck

Or that he has to go

Or boiler problems

Or parking tickets

Doesn't want help though

Too proud

There's

Not much love on the surface

But if you scratch away

It's probably hidden way down

Accidentally revealing itself

In the buying of a poetry book

Or a second hand van

Or heavy criticisms

In the guise of advice

Corridors

Dinner at Christmas

Maybe

In 78 years

It's really about

People he's known for ten

Lucky them

The rest of us

Can wait

We don't mind

That much

We love him

Cliff Britten

Rock

I can't sleep again

Just like you,

Our eyes fixed

Unblinking

Not really thinking

Both rolling and rocking

To take coke is shocking

You rock and roll fine

Without the white line

But you would of course

You wooden horse

Trust me

The Physician spoke gently

To his colleague

"Like me" he said

"If you find yourself

Carrying out a lobotomy

You'll need a fair amount of

Equipment

Most of this will be at the Hospital

In the theatre

I however have some

Instruments at home

In my kitchen

You see I do it for fun

I also carry a gun"

Madman

Mad vacant eyes stare into mine

I'm on the sofa, his face above mine

"I've told you never leave that fucking window open"

He is shaking me, he is calm but mental

A true maniac

He leaves

I think it through

There are bars on the window

No way in

It's 5.30 am

We're in the basement

It is so, so hot

He returns

"Whose fucking chess set is this?"

Pieces on a board

Set in study

The middle game

"It's all a fucking pose"

Chess pieces fly

I watch them slo—mo

Corridors

Black king and white queen

Buried by many pawns

No racism here at least

Knights and bishops reign supreme

On their black raft of the upturned board

The rooks, all four seek sanctuary

Beneath the table

Poetic coincidence

The end game

"Did you hear that?"

"No I did not hear anything"

But I know

There are bars on the windows

There's no way in

It's 5.30 am

We are in the basement

It's so very hot

Reg has lost it

In the hall

There is a shotgun

Peeping through the letterbox

Searching for a victim

Left and right

Up and down

A voice belongs to that gun

Owns it

Reg grabs the barrel

Wrestling the unseen enemy

Tug of war

Through the door

The gun goes off

The plaster flies

Reg screams

His hands are burned

Checkmate

I've had enough of this asylum

I want out

But there are bars on the windows

It's 5.30 am

We are in the basement

And it's all so hot.

This poem has been made into a short movie

And can be viewedhttp://vimeo.com/28861149

Good days

When the cymbals crash

And all the lights come on at once

Your head's cramped

And your face hurts

Everyone is waiting on you

Problems stack like dirty dishes

A simple thing

Making a phone call

Is like dying in a snake pit

When the walls move in

And the judges watch

Your eyes cry stinging tears

As the ceiling drops downward

On the paper staircase

That you designed

Over months of idleness

These are the good days

Count on them

Cliff Britten

Settle the Tab

Help me said the man

With the fish tank for a hand

The dwarf was not interested

His height

Was all that mattered

In this his shattered year

The end of a career

"I cannot sing, save me from

My own throat."

The diseased doctor put on his

Off—white coat

And then off again

The waiting room

Had already left

It had too much to do

The benches

Disappeared into the

Moving walls

And the screams

And the catcalls

Could be heard throughout

Corridors

This entire

Arid drought

The patched eye watched

Though saw nothing

Except red dust that

No one liked

It settled like

Snow on snow

But remained hot

Help me said the man

With the tab in his hand

Please lead me

From this hideous land

The patched eye itched and

Stared and stared

The priest and devil

Cared and dared

But not in that order

Dark lord of Mordor

Let normality open

And in it I'll slip

I grasp the wooden table

Only £2.50 for this trip

Cliff Britten

Mount Pleasant

Don't play on the roof

It's dangerous

Why won't you listen?

Look at you staring up at where

You were playing

Don't play on the roof

Do I have to tell you again?

Now you stare up there

Incredulous look on your face

Look at your arm

Bent at that extreme angle

Look at your leg

Snapped at the knee

White bone protruding

Don't play on the roof

Stop staring

A hundred feet is a long way

Globules of blood from your nose

A grin with red teeth

Corridors

Don't play on the roof

Don't stare

That huge crack

In your skull

Leaking brain fluid

You can't fly from Mount Pleasant

So don't play there

Cliff Britten

Corridors

Do you like my shoes?

They are all dead

All of them

Mozart, Lennon,

Hemingway, Byron

I could go on

Soon every single man jack of us

Will be joining them

Dead as doornails

Within a hundred years or so

Anyone on this planet

Talking the talk

Walking the walk

With their opinions

With their fashions

With their self—importance

Their mighty jobs

Their big houses

Them, their children

Grandchildren

All dead in a hundred years

Cliff Britten

So why go on about it so much

About what you think

What's right or wrong

What to eat

Wear, drink,

Read,

Who to seed

I don't care

What am I going to do about it?

All I have to say on the subject is

Do you like my new shoes?

The need

I feel the need

It comes from deep within

I must see her. I call

I go to her

She greets me like a long lost friend

Guides me to her discreet basement

The dimly lit room glints

Leads me to the waiting bed

Instructs me to remove my clothing

I will be back soon she teases

I wait in anticipation

She returns all in black

Small talk follows

She rubs the oils into my skin

It feels so good

The rhythm and motion

She is an expert

We are on first name terms

Then it is over

Cliff Britten

I dress

Money changes hands

£80 plus any extras

Not cheap for fifty minutes

I kiss her on both cheeks

Will you be back she asks

Oh yes I reply

It is so good

To get a facial

Inspired by Ewa

Sleep

She slept

As only she could

Breathing

Without movement

Not a sound

Her hair

Splayed

Around her shoulders

in glorious spread

Framing the beauty

Of perfect breasts

Legs parted slightly

In dark invitation

No morals

No guilt

No remorse

At peace

A face you could not hate

But the devil

Incarnate

Last poem of sorts

I can't write

And I'm scared

People used to say

Where does it all come from?

Where do you get the ideas?

I used to say

I don't know

It just comes

And it just did

Just come

But now it just doesn't

And I don't think I will

Be able to write

Again

I want to cry

I have lost a friend

Who ain't coming back

How could this happen?

Never try to write poems

Corridors

Or prose

If you have to think about it

It will sound wrong

Contrived

My last good poem sucked it all out

Of me

And now I sit here

Drinking beer

Breaking my own rule

My Golden rule

No one will ever see this

And it may be

The last thing

I ever write

And if so

I am sorry

But glad

If this

Is

it

Cliff Britten

Therapy

She said to me 'your poems

Are poignant, sad and real

They could certainly help people

People in therapy

I am a counsellor', she said

'I could use your poems

To heal people

People with emotional problems'

A lot of people say that to me

About my poems

But who's going to help me?

I only write them

Summer Time

Hoods and scarves

Cover faces

Black pupils

Reflect fire

Flaming husks of cars

Scream

In metallic pain

Sirens wail

Glass shatters

A woman jumps

From two floors high

Silhouetted in

Orange backdrop

Chased by smoke,

Static police watch

Moving fire spreads

Manufactured products

Corridors

Walk and disappear

Freed by looters

London, August, 7pm

A tiny blue baby bonnet

Sodden, lies by a drain

A shattered glass pane

Sticker intact

Reads

"More for your money"

The Witch

Witch's alley

300 yards long

But it stretched

Black forever

The task was set

The race was on

One 50 second run

To death or glory

The witch lived on the left

Half way up

In the theatre of shadows

Waiting for you

Ahead of you

Watching you

Daring you

Little boy

To run.

Behind you

Taunting laughing faces

Urging you

Pushing you

Corridors

Heart pounding

Run, run, run

The shadows thicken

Her house

Broken door

Cracked window

And her

Ugliness

Peering out at you

Legs turn to jelly

Dark door opening

Her toothless face

Run, run, run

She is upon you

Green sinewy hands

Grasping for your collar

You want to scream

She rules

Master of all

She eats small boys

Scrawny hand

Touches your neck

Nails scrape your skin

Drawing blood

Her hat is tall and black

She wears a cape

To wrap you in

The Witch, the Witch

Is real

She whispers

"You should not have

Come here little boy"

Tears well up

Eyes sting

Stumbling 20 yards to go

Run

The witch can only

Live in the alley

No further

A shared secret.

10 yards to

Reach the bend

Laughing faces await

Can't they see her?

Help me, help me

Please

Corridors

She pulls your collar

Rips it

Then

Free

Into the sunlight

The Witch has gone

Friends laugh

Slap your back

You grin a wide grin

Regain breath

Laugh, laugh and laugh

And can't stop laughing

Sailor

He sailed multi-coloured oceans

knew of the complexity of tides

The angle of sails

The shape of storms

He argued with the wind

Conversed with the stars

But now the grey clad sea

Screamed at him.

Relentlessly he fought it

Raged at it, hated it

Until

The waters called him

In a different voice.

Whispered to him gently

The night softened

Calm was upon him

Corridors

And as the blackness murmured

He became one with the waves

Lovers, mermaids and whores

Invited him

He gasped at this vision

Lungs bursting for air

And then down, down

The semblance of hands

Leading him home

To the sun and beyond

He had never been a sailor

Never learned to swim

Cliff Britten

Rules

"Religion is the opium of the masses"

So Marx said

People who live in round stones

Shouldn't wear glasses

Is what I say

A stitch in . . . . time

Is not relative

To Einstein

Do not put a cook

In a basket before hesitating

And never ever put

Icing on a camel's back

Without procrastinating

The boot wearer

He could cast or remove shadows

Depending on his stance, he could stand

In a thousand places, under an ocean

Or inside a mountain, nothing could phase

The boot wearer

Rider of sandstorms, sculptor of ice

Scanner of skies, teller of lies

No one denies the subtle disguise of

The boot wearer

Sound on gravel always the first sign

A darkening or at least a shift in the light

Air hanging heavier, a whisper

Soft promises, the smell of opium

The beat of a drum, you are struck dumb

And will succumb to

The boot wearer

Hypnotised by that form of leather on ankle

Dust lined creases that map the journey

To the river

Always to the river, under the willow

Forever to follow, behind the boot wearer

It's so bad

Ever since the dawn of man

Disasters have occurred

And horrific events taken place

September 11th

Sinking of the Titanic

Great fire of London

Holocaust

Late home for dinner

Columbine massacre

San Francisco earthquake

Socks left on bathroom floor

Black death

Aberfan

Barcelona trip cancelled

Apollo 13

The Great War

Piss on toilet seat

Hindenburg

World War 2

Please list them in order of gravitas

As you see fit

Cliff Britten

Woman act

Women are interesting

Especially women in bars

It's hard to strike up a conversation

But once in

They get really interesting

They play with their hair

Mimic your movements

Cross and uncross their legs

In such a way to keep you alert

They accept a drink

Just one

Tell you that you're strange,

Take another shot

Lick their lips

Touch the buttons on their shirts

Play with their ears

Tell you you're funny.

They will have . . . .

One more for the road

Corridors

Turn the subject to sex

Effortlessly

Talk quietly to draw you close

Breathe gently in your ear

Take your number

Tell you you're different

Hold your attention

Hold your stare

Hold your hand

Stumble to the last train home

Lose their nerve

Lose their memory

Lose your number

Question

I love her,

You love me

I like you a lot

A real lot

She don't love me

She likes me

She did love me

You've gone off me

I still like you

More than ever

I love her like a sister

I want you like a lover

She loves me like a brother

We don't have sex

With one another

What a load of

Fucking bother

Do you think?

We can recover?

Totem Pole

"This ain't no knife, this ain't no knife'

I stared at the urinal

He stared hard at my cock

I could feel his Indian eyes burning into me

He spoke from way up high

"This ain't no knife, this ain't no knife"

He kept staring at my cock

I put my cock away

"This ain't no knife"

He was right, no knife to be seen

Just his own huge cock standing

Totem pole

Not pretty, but impressive

"Piss off" . . . .

My mantra

When in America, don't take any shit from anyone

Especially in Denver

In a bus terminal

In a urinal

I left him admiring his pole

Cliff Britten

Sat down on my rucksack to read

"Catcher in the Rye" . . . for the third time

The page darkened

The shadow loomed

"This ain't no knife"

The mad man returns

For the second act

Intent, with the imaginary knife

Macbeth style

Lazy, one-dimensional security guards

Dancing on ice

My only saviours in this freak show

"You see that big Indian guy

He's mad, scary

He's got a knife that isn't there

I'm worried, he's huge

He worships Totem poles"

"Leave it to us"

They spoke as one

Slid over to him

A sauntering duo

Gliding him gently from the terminal

Exit stage left

Corridors

From this pantomime I am saved

At least . . . . until

Enter stage right

Another actor in a bright red number

He introduces himself to the security twins

His bloodied shirt speaks

"I just been stabbed by a crazy Indian"

He falls, his short appearance over

Cameo complete

The security boys lock gazes

Crass bookends

Shiny buttons, slack jaws

The crimson corpse beneath them

I should have played that role

They catch my eye

I start to cry

Catcher in the rye

Cliff Britten

6-15 pm

Three wet suits ride the surf

White arc above them

A barmaid fondles her glass

Eyes watch

From behind a paper

An old, old couple grip hands

A dog drinks Guinness

From a green dish

The sun sets

An orange Frisbee

On a blue satin cloth

6-16 pm

The glass breaks

The eyes fall

Hands part

The dog pukes

The wave crashes

Wipe-out

I am London

I live, I creep, I crawl

In endless style of rows

And rows of terraces I sprawl

Silver bullets shoot through deep arteries

Underground

Red corpuscles flow on roads

The sounds I make

I scream, I cry, I groan

Glass on glass on glass reflects

In the river that is my blood

It flows to escape me but never can

Constant in its fear of flood

I feel the radical change within

Car parks morphing into galleries of art

Depicting photos of empty

Car parks in the dark.

My single eye revolves, it spins

Observing all this moving mass

Inherent of its sins

Towers of Babylon

I have spawned

Corridors

Many flattened now

Though some remain

And then by man and crane

Reformed to live again

My concrete skin

Grey slab of life

Will be

The blank canvas for

The wild man with the knife

The new Picasso

Bleeds on me

Sprays my flesh with graffiti

My steely streets

Don't ever spurn

Some grim, they make

Your stomach churn

Yet teem with life at every turn

I am London

I live I creep I crawl

Steeped in centuries of

Fire, plague and war

Cliff Britten

I have endured it all

Pan out now

With designers' eye

You could not create me

You dare not try

This poem has been made into a short movie

And can be viewed
http://vimeo.com/28861149

Boredom

Sitting here

Looking at all the other things

That have not been done

Un-opened letters

Dirty washing

Beer—stained table

Smashed wineglass

Right in front of me

Less than a hand span away

I would rather

Measure the distance of it

Than clean it up

All that mess

While I sit here

Trying to write a

Worthless poem

For deaf ears and dull eyes

To deny

Cliff Britten

Two fat wood pigeons

Land on the fence

Start necking

Reminds me of

Little Red

They look directly at me

Hold my gaze

Then take off

They can barely fly

They are so fat

They think I'm

A crap poet

Two stone lions

Two broken lanterns

Why is everything in twos?

Picasso's "Bathers"

Jump to mind,

But that's in threes

Still can't write a decent poem

For nobody ever to read

It's sick, but I love it

As a man loves heroin

Corridors

Withdrawal time

Is upon me

Write something clever

Come on, write

Something

The guy next door is a jerk

He opens and shuts

His car doors over and over again

What is his problem?

O.C.D for a C.A.R

Finally he gets going

Starts the engine

Looks back at me

Through his rear view

Narrowing his eyes

Hurry up and piss off

Metal slug

Where does he go anyway?

5 mins and he'll be back with the

Door routine

How can anyone live with him?

With that!

Cliff Britten

I will write

Something profound

Not today though

Because I'm the coldest of all turkeys

Because I can't write

Because I am no poet

Because I don't love it

It ain"t heroin

I need a fix

One good line

I mean of poetry.

Don't get confused

This is where Bukowski

Would deliver the pay-off line

Maybe that was just mine

Devil of a decision

I have slept in a bed with Jesus Christ

And held the hand of his father

And after careful consideration

I know that I would rather

Clutch the hand of Satan

And attend all of his parties

He doesn't stand on ceremony

I know there will be Smarties

Tangerines and loads of drugs

Dark poetry read aloud

I could read out some of mine

I know he would be proud

Jesus and God have given me up

They just no longer listen

The devil's ears are all alert

His fiery eyes they glisten

They stare at me with great intent

I have joined his growing club

He doesn't really love me though

And "Therein lies the rub"

Girls I knew

Some of the girls I knew

Cheryl the Barbie doll

Tracey the gangster's moll

Chrissie, she loved Vic

Tisha the arty chic

Agnes the aggressive Scot

Mary the poshest of the lot

Gaynor so pretty but small

Louise too young and tall

Julie got all the way

Perfect, what can I say?

I just wish she'd stay

Watchmen

He was a scrawny man

Late 50s

Very clean

Silver hair

Decent teeth

Dressed smartly

Always stared at everyone

Especially women

At their legs

Their arses, their hair

Their tits

He made a funny sound

When someone grabbed his attention

A sucking sound

On his teeth

Gross

Took untold coke

Never shared it

Drank only Gin

Cliff Britten

With ice no mixer

Lots of Gins

Never shared those either

Gave everyone the creeps

No one said though

He had a bad look

In his eyes

And coke up his nose

Not a great mix

Same barstool every day

Boring bastard

Tight bastard

Never bought a drink

Never pulled

Never got drunk

Never left early

Just sat and watched

. . . .

And I watched him

Corridors

Flower

As you have left

I send you a text,

A photo

Of the cactus

In the bathroom

It has flowered.

From the dryness

Comes

Delicate pink and white petals

With red flashes

Swiftly without warning

Overnight

Bursting forth

A beautiful statement

Changing the room

You text back

"The cactus always flowers

Corridors

At this time of year

Just after the clocks go back,

Not enough light"

Oh! To be a cactus

Refined and reticent

In the sun and light

And now as nights draw in

When all else folds

It says its piece

What an attitude

In these dark times

Don't worry

My mum always used to worry about me

"Where you off to tonight"?

I felt it best to come clean

So I told her;

Meeting up with some friends

Drinking untold Jack Daniels

Onto a club

Bomb some speed

Neck a couple of pills

Dance non-stop for six hours

Lose 6lbs in weight

After party, more pills

Get amorous with new hot lady

Back to hers

Line of coke

Unprotected sex

Chill for a bit

Half a tab of acid

Purple ohm

Trip for 5 hours

Corridors

2 days no sleep

Sleep it off on Valium

Get home somehow

"Alright then" she'd say

"Be a good boy

Mind the road"

Cliff Britten

Living

When I sat by the valley of the rocks

Towering above the ocean

And the sun kissed my face

Death came up to me

He had pork pies and lemonade

A coloured picnic blanket

Checked pastel blue and pink

"Come closer to the edge

Look at the view" he urged

"Its all for you"

When I danced the trance of techno

A raving hedonist

Death came up to me

He had ecstasy and acid

Pretty pills and rainbow powder

Pupils huge and Adidas

"Feel the flow" he said

"It'll make you glow"

Corridors

When I jumped with parachute

Death came up to me

He glided by my side

With a purple box,

When opened

Terror

Spilled out

Shredding my nerves

He stayed with me

Followed me down

Laughing like some

Heinous clown

When I slept with a hundred girls

Death came up to me

He had weird, depraved ideas

All the shades of lust

A palette of obscenity

"You won't be using these" he said

He swept the condoms from the bed

When my mother died

Suddenly, shockingly

Far too young

Death came up to me

In undertaker's garb

All neat suit and sweet persona

With shiny coffin, red silk interior

With passive eyes

From an invisible page he read

"What the fuck are you doing?

Your Mothers dead!!!"

And now when I go anywhere

Death comes up to me

He has ideas and plans

Exciting, frightening

Enlightening

Infinite imagination

And a heavy slogan

"Roll up, roll up

To the daily grind

You're the next I have in mind"

Corridors

Thinking

I get to thinking a lot

And it hurts my head

It's pay back for my

Imagination

It's my curse

A simple object

To me is highly complex

A guitar or a butter dish

Interest me but

Can and do freak me out

When it gets to the real serious stuff

I have to stop myself

Thinking can get dangerous

Spiral out of control

I get the feeling

A lot of people

Don't think or care about anything

Cars, jars or Stars

Who has the curse?

Them or me?

Phone call

4.00 am . . . Phone call

My mum s been taken to hospital

57 years old

Her friend "asthma" called tonight

My dad won't say much, except

"Hurry"

I didn't like that word

On the way

I drive like Schumacher

On the final lap

Debate with God

Like Jeremy Paxman

Plead with, then ignore

Many red lights

6 miles in 6 minutes

World record?, No

Lost the race

Lost the debate with God

Lost my mum

Lost . . . .

Comedown

I stood on a crystal mountain

And held the earth

The music of all time passed by

My skin shivered and shook in pleasure

I smiled a thousand smiles

To a hundred faces

Invincible

And now the emerald blades cut deep

Pointed poison rain

Tearing my flesh

The music a throbbing mess

My body sweats and aches

I weep too often

Alone

Prop

Fleeting, floating

Amusing

Worrying, secretive

Confusing

Listening, caring

Disarming

Aloof, threatening

Alarming

Boring, brash

Proud

Flashy, freaky

Loud

Shoulder to cry on

Bed to lie on

The friends we need

Entrenched

Alone in the half dark

Dust particles float

Hard to breathe

Oppressive heat

Cramped and sweating

The constant din

The boom, boom, boom

Of men outside

Shouting, Bedlam

My eyes and skin itch

Difficult to see,

To move even

Trapped

Disobeyed orders

Caused this turmoil

I kneel

My face touching the floor

Pounding head

Close to tears,

Corridors

That will sting.

"Please help me

I can't do this"

Then

Someone is there

An arm

Around my shoulder

An ally

His voice

Calming

"Don't worry, it's okay,

Let's get out of here"

He leads me to the light

To the air

To sanity

To redemption

Salvation

It's not easy

Fitting a "Saniflo"

In the eaves

Of a loft

Night Visitor

The cockroach comes up the stairs

The new wooden ones

All polished, designer Oak steps

He makes a trip trappy noise

As his many feet try to gain purchase

On the shiny surface

He walks across my brand new carpet

Peers at me from the foot of the bed

Knowing eyes, they

Burn torment as a memory,

Straight to my gut

Tattooed, indelible.

Twitching

Antennae touch my face.

He is gross

We talk as usual

Mainly him

His voice

Nasal, droning, strident

He tells me

Where I've gone wrong

How cool he is in comparison

He is four feet long

Two feet wide

Glistening and revolting

Reeking

He asks if he can lie next to me

On the bed

No!!!!!!

You're a black cab

Driving, driving, driving

Taking, taking, taking

But I'm still the best thing in your life

He assures me

Stays, chatting for hours,

Feeling for secrets

Until I am a sobbing wreck,

The hairs on his legs bristle with this result

Then he leaves

Trip trapping

Back to "Hades"

His stench pervades

Cliff Britten

He leaves

A residue, a mess on the

Oak steps and the chrome door handle

He only comes

When I'm really down

He'll be back tomorrow

Physicality

Six hundred miles

Eight eyes divided into pairs of colour and shape

Nervous, hiding, hooded

Ballerinas behind curtains

Four mouths pursed tight

Speechless, biting bottom lips

To guard the unspoken word

Eight hands of different thickness, length and power

Wringing, fidgeting, drumming

Betraying calm

The miles diminish

The hands clutch beers

Form friendly gestures

The mouths chew sandwiches

Smile, show teeth, different shades of white

The eyes search out other eyes

And meet approvingly

Pupils dilate

Ink on blotting paper

Miles are completed

Journey done

The hands shake other hands

Pat backs

Clutch phones, take numbers

The eyes enquire, sad but creased

As laughter emerges

The mouths utter speech

Exchange pleasantries, goodbyes

Kiss cheeks, grin

Four people bond

Over six hundred miles

Across 2 countries

Over a table

On a train

Corridors

The speed of life

Born
Slapped

School
Trapped

Job
Girls
Fun

Marry
Mortgage
Done

Parent
Stress

Mortgage paid
Stress less

Grandparent
Thrilled

Retire
Chilled

Illness
Groan

Worsen
Moan

Dead
And
Finally
Chilled
To the bone

Warning

And as the World slept

Under a blanket of lead

Out of the silence there came

A warning

That was screamed

In a frightened voice

Pleading

That it should not be done

The World did not listen

It held its ears

And the warning vanished

In the hollow sky

And it was done

And the Earth wept

And wept

And wept

We all did

Register

Britten   (that's me)

Coles

Davis   (my best mate)

Dingley

Flatman

Glyde

Harris

Hole

Isaacson

Keely

Leach

Mead

Moat

Rolt

Stone

Tippett

Watson

Widdows

And Wilkinson

Velux

Jarred from sleep

Again to face the clock

Stark digital display

Electric blue neon

Demanding my eyes

3:33 the misery numbers

Behind me I feel the shadow

Fixed into the wall

Its creator the "Velux" window

I sense its blackness, malevolence

Power and shape

Taunting, reaching

"Velux" window, position of moon

Time, motion, clouds

Impair me

Am I insane?

A whirr, a click

The digits change

3:.34 but the shadow remains

Cliff Britten

The Bell

I was born and cast a beautiful bell

Forged by men who loved me

I never rang a sombre knell

Brightly I chimed on Sundays

But I possessed a fatal flaw

My casting not quite right

Upon me dealt a hand so raw

A crack on me to blight

My singing now is dirge and gloom

A tearful sad lament

The crack is like an empty room

My shape is warped and bent

More sadness yet for me in store

Two robbers saw my worth

They took me from my space, my core

My noble place of birth

Corridors

Now my voice forever droll

Can proudly sing no more

Those robbers took from me, my soul

And the heart I had, they tore

Think! Thieves before you melt me down

Do not for greed or gain

But recast me high upon that place

To sing a new refrain

Cliff Britten

Ketamine

You're a really great friend of mine

And next time we meet

I am going to let you know just why

We are so, so close

Just a phone call

And there you are

How we warm each other

I heat you first and then you me

You never disappoint

We never argue or fight

Funny thing is though

Our times together are a little weird

Warped and terrific

We are going to meet right now actually

I am going to tell you exactly what you do to me

If I can, if you let me

Are you ready?

I am

Vamos

Grabbing the back of my hair again

Tugging gently

I love that, you know it

Numb . . . is my name, I think

Although thinking is not that easy at the mo'

Numb but pleasant is my full name

Things will shift, are shifting . . . .

Still shifting

The corner of my eye, both eyes

Catch the shift

The curtains move slightly

The Ants' theatre production

Gets underway

What are they up to?

Forget about them

Let's talk about us

We need music

"I tunes" will bring us

"Ceremony" Joy division

"Ceremony" or is it "Cemetery"?

Or memory?

I can't remember a cemetery

STOP IT! STOP IT!

What are the Ants up to?

What goes on behind the curtain?

Production will start soon

Play out . . . .

The Ants' ceremony

With no memory

That can't work

They need to remember the lines

It will be a flop, not enough seats in the house

Just a sofa and one swivel chair

Not enough revenue for Ants

They need bums on seats

They need to expand

Expanding Ants!!!,

STOP IT! Please. No Ants I said

Are you my friend or what?

I am done in, you have done me in

Let's not go there

My heads warm,

Corridors

Swimming is fine

Swimming in fire

Shift . . . . shift again

"Ceremony"

Great tune

I never knew this track was so good

Track?

Why is it a track?

I've lost track

Let's track back

Trick track

You make me laugh out loud

Told you we were friends

Let's not do the "Ant" thing again

Let's count feet

I have two and you have

Zero

But there are four feet here

Or is that a pair of shoes?

Four feet is just over a metre

You see

Cliff Britten

You can be funny when you try

Just don't talk about the Ants okay!

Shift . . . . Shift again

I know you will leave me soon

And so will the ants and the feet

And the track and the room

Ceremony and memory

The warders of the brain

Will be but a fume

It's all so cosy

Promise to come back soon

Dylan

I was listening to Dylan in the park

On a cassette player

All doom and gloom

Him not me

She crossed the road

All pink puffer and ponytail

Eighteen years old

Long legs, sticky out ears

Bright red lips and a

Priceless scowl

She'd never ever heard of Dylan

Who was trying his best

On the blues harp

"What's your fucking problem"

She screamed and

Walked off wiggling

The tightest butt on the planet

Bob and I were gob smacked

Sometimes

When the idiots scream

And the ugly frown their frowns

The midget howls alone in an unjust sleep

While the fat man struggles to stand

The murderer grips his seventh neck

And the terror spreads around

As madmen walk with fists in mouths

And we watch on frozen ground

This show is here on earth, no doubt

Please cover my eyes

When the freaks freak out

There can be solace

Somewhere

Though

For

In the steel hard metal

Of the cold gun barrel

And the shape of the bullet

Lies peace

To write

Writing a poem

Can take it out of you

But sometimes it's like

A deep cut to a thick vein

With a sharp, sharp blade

The blood flows clean and bright

Rich and clear

Painless

On and on it spurts

Red river, endless

Filling page after page

Leaving its mark

Presence felt

Not everyone likes it

But it can't be denied

Other times though

It's like this

In Chicago

In Chicago

A black face said

"Shoe shine mister?"

In Chicago

I said "No I'm no tourist"

In Chicago

He said, "no charge mister

You from London?"

In Chicago

He's real friendly

In Chicago

My boots are buffed

He talks and talks

My boots shine and shine

In Chicago

He asks for twenty dollars

In Chicago

I told him

"I'm no tourist, you said no charge"

Corridors

In Chicago

He shows me his knife

In Chicago

I was mugged

In Chicago

My boots look amazing

Meeting

In a park, we met, at a table

Sixty-four squares of black and white between us

You never spoke just grunted, shifting pawns

With oversized hands

You ignored my opening gambit

Repelled my Sicilian attack

Yes, you were good, very good

Though not in conversation

Uncompromising tight defence

My knights and bishops nudged your army

To bond and befriend

But you, aggressive and silent

Tortured my queen, surrounded my rook

Killed my king and destroyed me

And in winning this battle

You refused to smile

Showtime

Strings broken one by one

A useless marionette

Sad eyes and a single tear

Held by God?

Partly at least, lovers have left

And death hangs around us all

Uninvited

Floating in a windowless black theatre

No crowd to please

I want to talk, to be heard, to matter

But I am a puppet

And God the puppeteer

I am . . . severed at both ends

I have no act

But I have one friend

One legacy

This pen I hold . . .

I feel like this

So get it told

Cliff Britten

Kiln

It's all about heart really

Yours the size of a hot air balloon

Floating free

On a cloudless sky

Mine, a narrow cul-de-sac

One-way street

Double red line

Please drive carefully through this village

Warm me

I am a cup from the kiln unfired

The poison flows from small holes

Fire me, fire me

Two thousand Fahrenheit

Shine

Glaze my soul

Balloon

In my head

I draw a heart shaped balloon and float it to you

In my head

You have eager arms outstretched

Smiling that smile of yours

In my head

You can't wait to caress that balloon

You run towards it

In my head

I shout, "Be careful that balloon is delicate"

More like a bubble, so fragile.

In my head

You gather that balloon so gently

That vulnerable bubble balloon

And hold it close to your own heart

It doesn't break . . .

In your head though

There is no balloon

Snow

Look at all the dead people

Under the snow

Their graves look pretty

Do you think they care?

"Oh the snow has settled nicely on my cross

Giving it that Christmassy feel"

And

"Look at my headstone

The blanket of whiteness

Really sets it off

Against the green moss"

And then

"The way the white powder

Has banked up against my

Tombstone is a joy to see

Don't you just love it, when it snows

We love this look"

Babies and Nazis

I saw them, yellow circles

Surrounding bright red circles

Kaleidoscope

Moving rings that drank medication

100 red circles

100 yellow bands encompassing

Baby chicks, delicate patterns a

Beautiful sight of symmetry and nature

When the red dishes were pulled up

The beaks rose in unison, begging

Dishes out of reach though

The yellow rings disappeared

Fractured format

Leaving a mass of patchy yellow carpet

My thought from the doorway of the hanger

Where the chicks lived

Were . . .

I am here to help you chicks

I am here to learn

To save your vulnerable souls

My first view of them inspiring

"Come in" he said

'I will teach you"

Walking into the hanger with bucket trailing

Instructs me to follow

He stoops, picks up some dead chicks

Places them all too gently into his bucket

"Hey:" . . . . I shouted

You are trampling them with your boots

Two or three chicks trodden in the dust

Beneath his Nazi feet

Then more

With every step came death

"Hey you stop, you are killing them!"

I cried, ... "Please stop"

"It happens" he said

"You'll learn"

Are you okay?

My friends phone me

"Are you okay?"

"How are things?"

"Things are okay, I'm good"

I lie

I hate lying to my friends

But I don't want to

Depress people

So I just lie instead

"Everything's fine"

I wish they would stop ringing

"No I didn't mean that!"

Please ring

"I'm fine"

The lonely mask

I am here, I have been here for many years

Discarded, forgotten, alone

But what a vision I am still

Blue plumage sprays above golden form

Diamonds encrust my hollowed eyelets

Yes I have eyes or at least holes

Vacant, barren spaces

I have no ears to hear though

No mouth to kiss or tell

No nose to smell fine perfume

No legs to stand and posture

No hands to touch or feel a face

Wear me please, once more, wear me

Shake free the oppressive dust

Pull my black ribbons tight

Let me feel your flesh

Your sweet breath

Your eyes become mine

Let us embrace, dance, sing

What a hedonistic pair we made

What heady days, when we were one

Inspired by

Trinity Rose

Shortlist

I thought

I might try to write

A poem about happiness

What makes me happy

I get criticised for

Being too dark

Too morbid

So I am going to try

Really hard to write an

Uplifting poem

Of all the things

That make me happy

Here goes

Horses . . .

Cliff Britten

Incongruous

Candle lit dinners

Both of you are sinners

Seven year itch

Which one is the bitch?

Find another lover

Don't think I'll bother

Flowers on the bed

Bullets in the head

10-second symmetry

Life is here,

Chatter in the car

Five seconds

"Are we there yet dad?"

Three seconds

"I need the loo dad!"

Zero seconds

The blanket of fog hangs nonchalantly

It manages though, in its vaporised malevolent state

To create death from life, the axis of macabre symmetry

Zero seconds

Crunch of steel

Three seconds

Twisted metal

Five seconds

Life has gone

Silence . . .

Inside art illustrations and front cover photograph by Clifford Britten